THE
BROXBOURNE SCHOOL
LIBRARY RESOURCE CENTRE

LEARN AND SERVE

High Road Broxbourne
Herts EN10 7DD

NATURAL DISASTERS

Artist:

Nick Hewetson was educated in Sussex
at Brighton Technical School, and studied
illustration at Eastbourne College of Art. He has
since illustrated a wide variety of children's books.

Consultant:

John Cooper is a geologist and Keeper of
the Booth Museum of Natural History in Brighton.
He has written several books on geological topics,
including dinosaurs and volcanoes and has acted as
consultant on many others.

Editor:

Karen Barker Smith

Created, designed and produced by
**THE SALARIYA BOOK
COMPANY LTD**
25 Marlborough Place,
Brighton BN1 1UB

ISBN 0 7500 2922 6

Published in 1999 by
Macdonald Young Books,
an imprint of Wayland
Publishers Ltd,
61 Western Road,
Hove BN3 1JD

You can find Macdonald
Young Books on the internet
at:http://www.myb.co.uk

A CIP catalogue record for this
book is available from the
British Library.

Repro by Modern Age

Printed in Singapore.

Author:

Jenny Vaughan lives in London.
She has written and edited children's books on a
variety of subjects. These include several science
titles and books on dinosaurs and other
prehistoric information books. Her special
interest is the environment and the
natural world.

Series creator:

David Salariya
was born in Dundee, Scotland,
where he studied illustration and
printmaking. He has illustrated
a wide range of books and has
created many new series of books
for publishers in the UK and
overseas. In 1989 he established
The Salariya Book Company.
He lives in Brighton with
his wife, the illustrator
Shirley Willis, and
their son.

FAST FORWARD

NATURAL DISASTERS

Written by
JENNY VAUGHAN

Illustrated by
NICK HEWETSON

Created and designed by
DAVID SALARIYA

MACDONALD YOUNG BOOKS

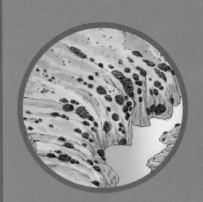

Contents

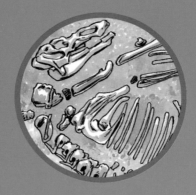

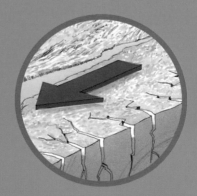

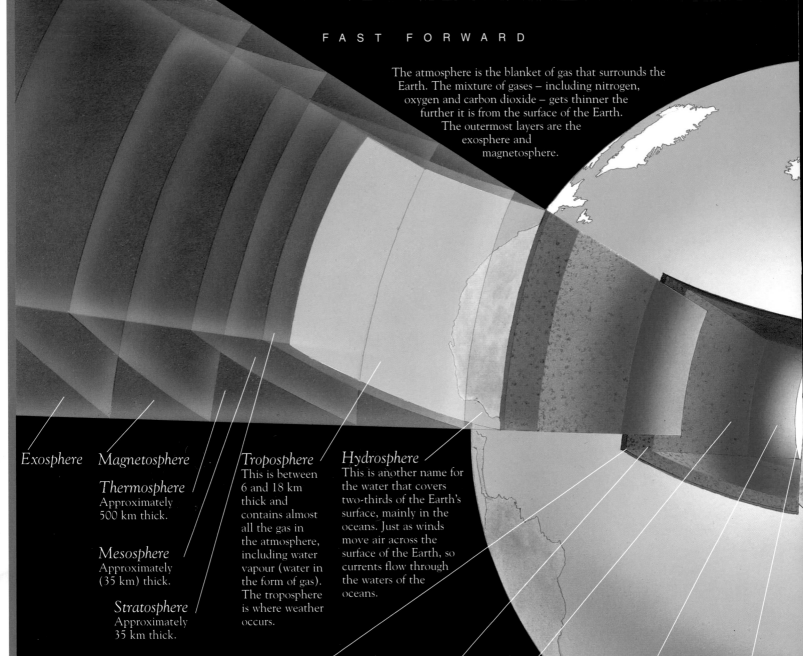

The atmosphere is the blanket of gas that surrounds the Earth. The mixture of gases – including nitrogen, oxygen and carbon dioxide – gets thinner the further it is from the surface of the Earth. The outermost layers are the exosphere and magnetosphere.

Exosphere   *Magnetosphere*

Thermosphere
Approximately 500 km thick.

Mesosphere
Approximately (35 km) thick.

Stratosphere
Approximately 35 km thick.

The area of atmosphere above 80 km is also referred to as the ionosphere because the air is full of electrically charged particles called ions.

Troposphere
This is between 6 and 18 km thick and contains almost all the gas in the atmosphere, including water vapour (water in the form of gas). The troposphere is where weather occurs.

Hydrosphere
This is another name for the water that covers two-thirds of the Earth's surface, mainly in the oceans. Just as winds move air across the surface of the Earth, so currents flow through the waters of the oceans.

Crust
The Earth's crust is the tough, outer surface of the Earth. On average, it is about 30 km thick under land, but under mountains it can reach 70 km. It is only about 7 km thick beneath the ocean.

Lithosphere and Asthenosphere
Beneath the crust lies the Earth's mantle. The outermost layer of the mantle is attached to the crust. The two together are called the lithosphere and are about 100 km thick. Below these is the next layer of the mantle, the asthenosphere.

Mantle
The mantle makes up about nine-tenths of the Earth. It extends 2,800 km down to the Earth's outer core. The asthenosphere is made up of hot, soft rock, over which the plates of the lithosphere move.

Outer Core
Beneath the mantle lies the Earth's outer core, which is about 2,250 km thick. No one has ever seen it, but scientists believe it is mainly made up of iron and nickel. Temperatures in the outer core are about 5,500°C. The metal here is molten (liquid).

Inner Core
The inner core is also metal and is about 1,220 km thick. Scientists believe its temperature is probably about 6,000°C. Metal at such a high temperature would normally be molten, but the huge amount of pressure from the other layers of the Earth means it is solid.

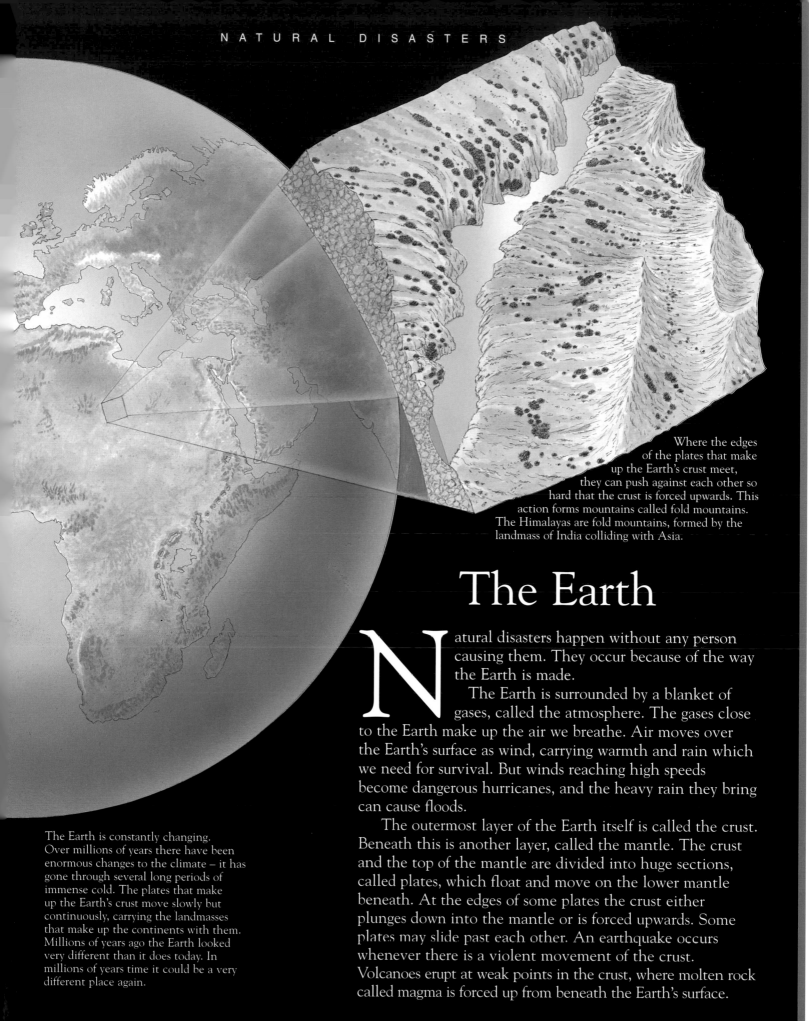

Where the edges of the plates that make up the Earth's crust meet, they can push against each other so hard that the crust is forced upwards. This action forms mountains called fold mountains. The Himalayas are fold mountains, formed by the landmass of India colliding with Asia.

The Earth is constantly changing. Over millions of years there have been enormous changes to the climate – it has gone through several long periods of immense cold. The plates that make up the Earth's crust move slowly but continuously, carrying the landmasses that make up the continents with them. Millions of years ago the Earth looked very different than it does today. In millions of years time it could be a very different place again.

The Earth

Natural disasters happen without any person causing them. They occur because of the way the Earth is made.

The Earth is surrounded by a blanket of gases, called the atmosphere. The gases close to the Earth make up the air we breathe. Air moves over the Earth's surface as wind, carrying warmth and rain which we need for survival. But winds reaching high speeds become dangerous hurricanes, and the heavy rain they bring can cause floods.

The outermost layer of the Earth itself is called the crust. Beneath this is another layer, called the mantle. The crust and the top of the mantle are divided into huge sections, called plates, which float and move on the lower mantle beneath. At the edges of some plates the crust either plunges down into the mantle or is forced upwards. Some plates may slide past each other. An earthquake occurs whenever there is a violent movement of the crust. Volcanoes erupt at weak points in the crust, where molten rock called magma is forced up from beneath the Earth's surface.

7

Death of the Dinosaurs

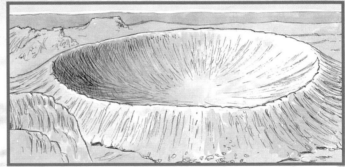

Dinosaurs were reptiles, a little like the reptiles of today, such as lizards and turtles. This means that they were probably cold-blooded and needed the sun's heat to warm their bodies and give them energy. Dinosaurs lived on Earth for nearly 200 million years. There were many different types, from small, swift ones to heavy lumbering plant-eaters and savage hunters. Suddenly, 65 million years ago, they disappeared – why?

One theory is that they were killed when an asteroid crashed into the Earth from space. This would have caused earthquakes and volcanic eruptions that would have thrown up so much dust that the world was dark for months. There would have been a long, cold winter which the cold-blooded dinosaurs could not survive. They would have died out, leaving only creatures such as the warm-blooded birds and mammals to survive.

A crater off the coast of Mexico (see map, below) shows that an asteroid (small planet) or meteorite (rock) landed there from space about 65 million years ago. It was so big it would have caused an explosion as powerful as 10,000 nuclear bombs, destroying everything up to 500 km away.

As the asteroid burned, the thick cloud of poisonous gas and dust it made could have caused a change in the climate. However, some scientists think the climate was getting colder anyway, so the asteroid and volcanic eruptions just made this happen faster.

crater

MEXICO

Pacific Ocean

Meteor Crater, in Arizona, in the US (above), was formed some time in the last 50,000 years when a meteorite hit the Earth. The crater is 1,200m wide.

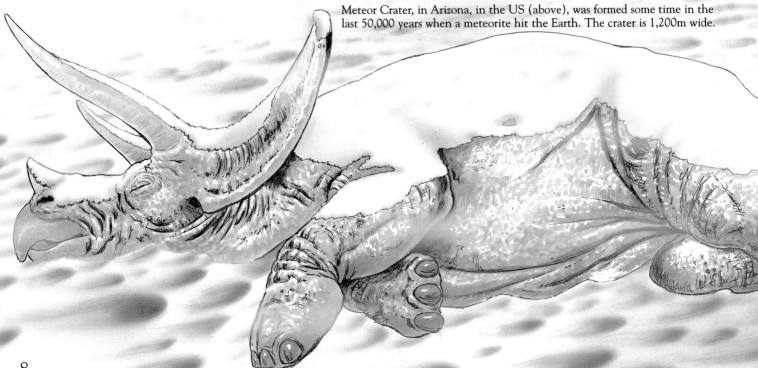

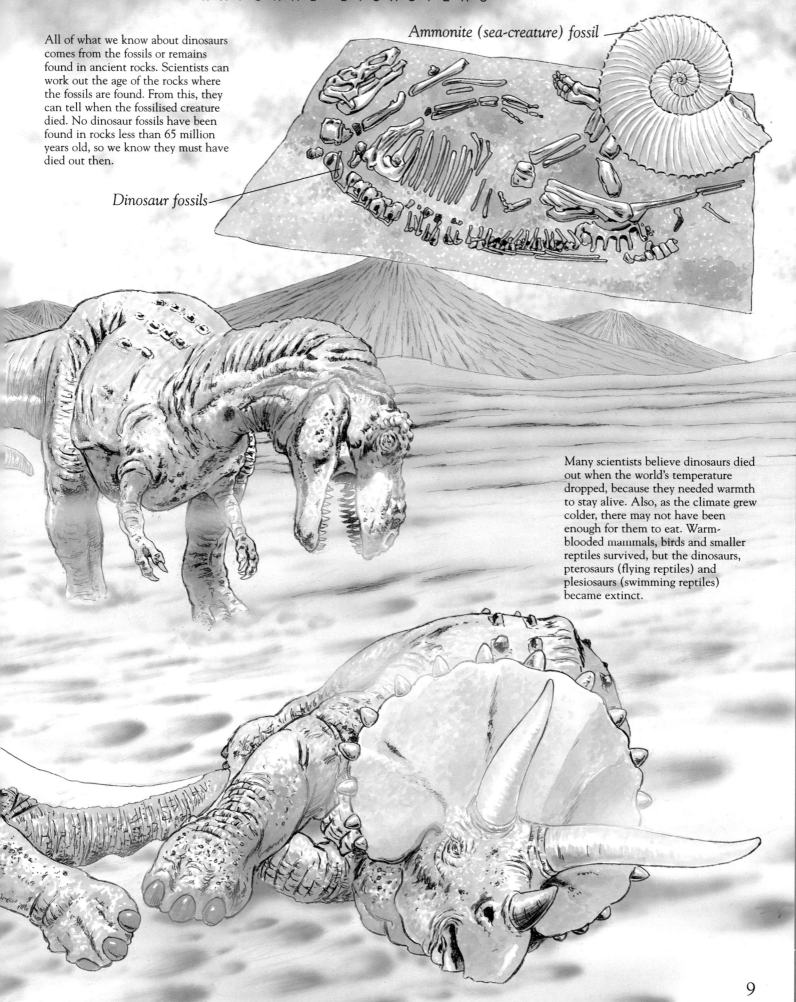

All of what we know about dinosaurs comes from the fossils or remains found in ancient rocks. Scientists can work out the age of the rocks where the fossils are found. From this, they can tell when the fossilised creature died. No dinosaur fossils have been found in rocks less than 65 million years old, so we know they must have died out then.

Ammonite (sea-creature) fossil

Dinosaur fossils

Many scientists believe dinosaurs died out when the world's temperature dropped, because they needed warmth to stay alive. Also, as the climate grew colder, there may not have been enough for them to eat. Warm-blooded mammals, birds and smaller reptiles survived, but the dinosaurs, pterosaurs (flying reptiles) and plesiosaurs (swimming reptiles) became extinct.

9

Pompeii:
The eruption of Vesuvius

At about midday on 24 August in AD 79, the Roman city of Pompeii was destroyed by one of the most famous volcanic eruptions ever. Pompeii was a busy port on the coast of Italy and nearby were two other towns, Stabiae and Herculaneum. All three were close to Mount Vesuvius, a volcano that was believed to be extinct (would never erupt again). No one in the surrounding towns was prepared for Vesuvius's eruption.

Although this disaster happened nearly 2,000 years ago, we know a lot about it because a man called Pliny the Younger, aged 17, wrote an eye-witness account. A 'black and dreadful' cloud, full of flames, made the area 'as dark as a sealed room without lights'. Small stones started to fall from the sky like hail. Some people tried to run away while others shut themselves in their houses. Then a cloud of burning gas and ash swept down the mountain. Pliny reported that it spread out 'like a flood', burning and suffocating everyone in its path. At Herculaneum, it killed thousands more on the beach as they tried to escape.

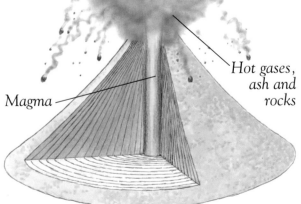

Magma

Hot gases, ash and rocks

How a volcano works
Volcanoes form mostly at the edges of the plates that make up the Earth's crust. Pressure from the mantle beneath forces molten rock, called magma, towards the Earth's surface, forming a volcano. When magma reaches the Earth's surface, it is called lava. As the volcano erupts, lava, hot gases and ash pour out of its crater. Some eruptions are violent explosions, while in others lava pours down the side of the volcano, hardening into rock as it cools.

After the Eruption

All three towns of Pompeii, Herculaneum and Stabiae were completely buried in ash and rocks. Around 16,000 people died in Pompeii. The eruption blew away the whole centre of Mount Vesuvius. Pompeii and the other towns were almost forgotten until, in the mid-1700s, Herculaneum and Pompeii began to be excavated.

Today, visitors can see Pompeii's ruined buildings and walk along the ancient streets. The pictures painted on the walls and even graffiti written long ago can now be seen. Visitors can imagine being in Pompeii the day it was destroyed.

In the 1860s, an archaeologist named Guiseppe Fiorelli found a way of making life-size models of people whose bodies were buried in ash in Pompeii.

The bodies of people buried in the eruption had rotted away, leaving a hollow space in the hardened ash. Fiorelli poured plaster of Paris into this space (left).

When the plaster became solid, Fiorelli chipped away at the ash. This would uncover the plaster cast of someone who had died on 24 August, AD 79 (left).

Earthquakes

The city of San Francisco, in the United States, lies close to a crack in the Earth's crust called the San Andreas fault. Faults are often found at the edges of the plates that make up the crust. The rocks along a fault may become jammed against each other and not move for many years. But eventually pressure builds up and the rocks suddenly break apart. The edges of the fault move violently, causing an earthquake.

Today there are strict rules to make sure buildings in San Francisco are as safe as possible in an earthquake. But these rules did not exist in 1906, when the worst earthquake ever to hit the United States happened there.

The earthquake of 1906 had its epicentre (centre at ground level) in the San Francisco area. Tremors (shaking) may spread for hundreds of kilometres.

Epicentre at San Francisco

If vibrations from an earthquake are moving through loose soil, sand or soft rock, the shaking ground starts to behave almost like a liquid. Buildings on ground that has 'liquefied' in this way topple over or sink (left).

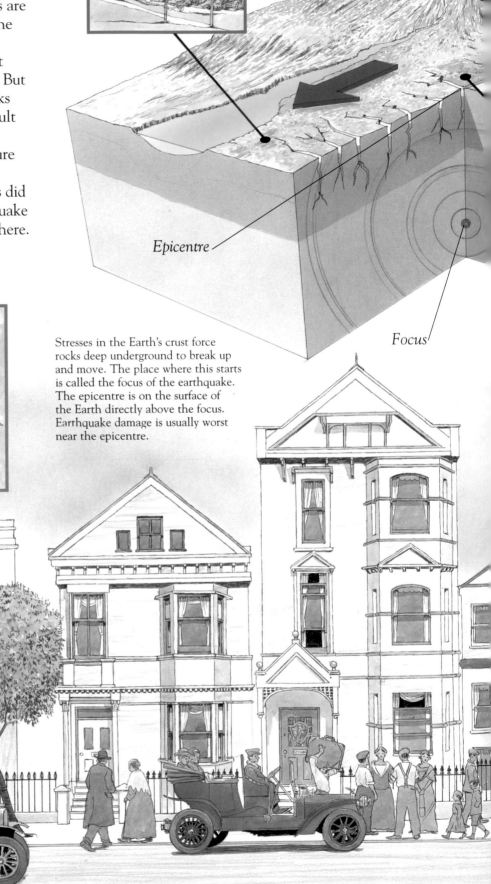

Epicentre

Focus

Stresses in the Earth's crust force rocks deep underground to break up and move. The place where this starts is called the focus of the earthquake. The epicentre is on the surface of the Earth directly above the focus. Earthquake damage is usually worst near the epicentre.

An earthquake in mountains can trigger a landslide or an avalanche (right) that will bury everything below it. An avalanche caused by an earthquake in Peru, in 1970, killed almost everyone in a town of 20,000 people. Only 92 survived.

n Francisco
arthquake

isaster struck San Francisco early in the morning on 18 April 1906. The roads began to move up and down like waves and houses began to sway. People were actually thrown eir beds. Buildings came tumbling any were made of wood and they n on fire. The water mains were and fire-fighters could not put out es. They tried blowing up buildings he fires spreading, but this made vorse. Thousands of people were left ss and had to leave the city or camp he open. Over 500 were killed.

Collapsing buildings are not the only dangerous result of an earthquake. Fires spread among damaged buildings (left), especially if gas and oil pipes are broken. Water supplies may be disrupted and the many homeless people will need shelter and food. It is important to get rescue teams to an area struck by an earthquake as quickly as possible.

Hurricanes and Cyclones

Hurricanes are violent storms that form over the warm seas of the Caribbean. They start life as thunder storms as warm, wet air close to the sea rushes upwards, forming heavy clouds. These storms may band together, creating fast-moving winds that circle around a still centre or 'eye'. A typical hurricane can be about 600 km across. The scientific name for one of these storms is a tropical cyclone because they are common in the tropics – the area around the Equator. The name hurricane is used for these storms when they occur in America. In the Western Pacific they are called typhoons, while in the Indian Ocean they are cyclones.

Water vapour (water in the form of gas) in the rising air condenses to form thick clouds.

Torrential rain falls beneath

Upward spiral of wind

The eye of the storm

Inside a tropical cyclone

A tropical cyclone forms as warm, damp air rises from near the surface of the sea. Winds of cool air blow in beneath it. The spinning motion of the Earth makes these winds travel upwards in a spiral reaching around 50 kilometres per hour, with gusts of 360 kilometres per hour. In the middle of this swirling mass there is a calmer column of warm air, moving upwards and cooling at the same time. This is the eye of the storm.

Cool air billows out from the top of the storm and forms a huge circle of cloud.

Living with Storms

Living through a tropical cyclone can be terrifying. Wind flattens buildings and trees. Waves more than 8 m high crash in from the sea and torrents of rain cause floods and landslides. In rich countries, people can be prepared for a tropical cyclone. They have strong homes and can make them even stronger, by nailing boards over windows and doors. If things become really dangerous, good transport and organisation helps people get away from the storm. But in poorer countries, things are more difficult. There are usually less materials and equipment available for preparing for the storms, building shelters or for rescue services.

In 1991, a hurricane hit the coast of Florida, in the United States. Huge waves crashed into southern Miami and caused an enormous amount of damage (left).

Plagues

Locust

Colorado beetle

Mosquito

The word 'plague' usually refers to the deadly disease that is spread by the fleas that live on rats. It is also called the Black Death. In the mid-1300s, it killed approximately 30 million people in Europe and many more in Asia and Africa. Half the people in England died – there were so many bodies that people had to be buried in pits instead of proper graves. There were two kinds of plague. The most common was bubonic plague. It caused a fever and dark swellings in a person's armpits and groin. Those affected died within a few days. Pneumonic plague affected the lungs and it killed a person within hours. The Black Death in the 14th century was the worst outbreak of plague ever known. Today, the plague is only found in the poorest parts of the world.

Diseases that attack crops can do almost as much harm as ones that directly kill people. In the 1840s, potato blight, a disease caused by a fungus, killed potato crops in Europe (above). In Ireland, people depended heavily on potatoes for food. Without them, about a million people died of starvation or became so weak they died of other diseases. It became known as the Irish Potato Famine. A million more people left Ireland and never returned.

The Bible tells the story of how Moses led the people of Israel from slavery in Egypt. Before they left, ten 'plagues' took place. Some were plagues of pests, others were diseases. One of the plagues was of frogs. When the frogs died there followed a plague of lice and a plague of flies. Scientists and historians believe the lice and flies arrived to feed on the bodies of the dead frogs.

Epidemics

When a disease spreads among a large number of people it is called an epidemic. Different diseases spread in different ways. Many are caused by micro-organisms (tiny living things). There are two main types of these – viruses and bacteria. Some bacteria are spread when creatures such as lice or fleas bite one person and then go to another. Bubonic plague is an example of this. Other bacteria are spread through water or air, or even by contact between people. Many diseases caused by bacteria can be cured using drugs called antibiotics. A scientist named Alexander Fleming discovered the first antibiotic, penicillin, in 1928.

Some diseases are caused by smaller organisms called viruses. Influenza (flu), for example is caused by a virus. It is spread by people sneezing, coughing, breathing and touching each other.

Sometimes the word 'plague' is used to refer to a large number of pests. In Africa and Asia, plagues of locusts occasionally swarm over farmland, eating all the crops. Plagues of rats eat stored grain and may carry disease. A plague of Colorado beetles can destroy whole fields of potato plants, while mosquitoes spread the disease malaria.

Robert Koch (pictured above) was the scientist who discovered that the bacterium that causes cholera comes from human bodily waste. Cholera spreads when people drink water polluted with this waste. Koch also studied diseases such as tuberculosis (TB), bubonic plague and malaria.

Around 1800, Dr Edward Jenner discovered that people were immune from the disease smallpox if they had already had another, less dangerous disease called cowpox. Jenner had the idea of injecting people with cowpox so they became safe from smallpox. He called this procedure a vaccination. Worldwide vaccination has caused smallpox to disappear completely.

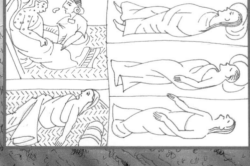

In the 16th century, Spanish invaders infected Aztecs with smallpox. Sketches from that period (right) show the suffering the disease caused.

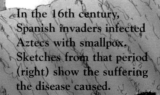

AIDS (acquired immune deficiency syndrome) is a killer disease caused by a virus. It can be passed on through sex with an infected person or through infected blood.

In 1918, just after the First World War, there was an epidemic of Spanish flu. More than 40 million people died from it all over the world.

'Mad cow disease' comes from some types of cattle food. It damages cattles' brains and kills them. People who eat meat from these cattle are in danger of getting the disease themselves.

Fear of Floods

Rivers provide fresh water which every living thing needs to stay alive. A river can be used by families, farmers, industries and as a valuable transport route for boats to carry goods and people. It is for these reasons that villages, towns and cities often develop near rivers.

Two mighty rivers flow through China: the Huang He and the Yangtze. Millions of people live close by them, working in factories and farming. One of the most important crops in China is rice, which grows in paddy fields – areas of land covered in ankle-deep water. But living and working near rivers can be dangerous. When water from melting snow pours into a river, or after heavy rains, there is a serious chance of flooding.

The Yangtze River floods in 1991

Most seriously affected provinces of China

HENAN

JIANGSU

ANHUI

SICHUAN

HUBEI

Shanghai

YANGTZE RIVER

ZHEJIANG

HUNAN

GUIZHOU

24

Earthquakes beneath the sea can cause huge tidal waves or tsunamis (below). Out at sea, these are low, very broad waves. But close to the shore, they can rise to over 30 m high and travel inland at 600 kilometres per hour. In 1998, tidal waves hit the coast of New Guinea in the Pacific Ocean, killing around 2,000 people.

Destroyed by Water

When the Yangtze River flooded in 1931, over three million people were killed. In 1954, floods on the Yangtze killed 30,000. The 1990s have seen six serious floods there and they seem to be happening more often. The floods in 1998 were the worst since 1954. So many people live along the Yangtze that saving them was a huge problem. Millions of homes and factories were destroyed, farm animals drowned and crops were ruined. Soldiers spent weeks helping to build up dykes along the river and getting people to higher ground. In spite of this, about 5,000 people died.

27

Weather Forecasting

When dangerous weather is on its way, being prepared can save lives. Weather forecasting has been studied for hundreds of years. In the past, meteorologists (scientists who study weather) used simple thermometers to measure air temperature and barometers to measure air pressure. Information from these helped them to predict the weather. But the predictions were often not very accurate so heavy rain and violent storms could still take people by surprise.

Today, meteorologists use modern thermometers, barometers and other instruments to predict weather changes more accurately. Their studies include the movement of cloud, speed and direction of wind and the amount of rainfall. Measurements like these are taken at thousands of weather stations all over the world – from oil rigs at sea, ships and weather buoys. Aircraft and helium-filled balloons carry instruments high into the atmosphere to take meteorological readings. Radar is used to see where and how much rain is falling. Satellites above the Earth beam back photographs of clouds and information about weather systems around the planet. All this data is collected at weather centres and used to make weather forecasts.

Weather balloon

Barometer

Weather buoys have been used since the 1970s. They drift over the oceans measuring temperature, wind speed, air pressure and humidity. Their transmitters send information from their instruments to satellites, which then beam them back to weather centres on land. Computers use this information to help forecast the weather.

Weather buoy

At weather centres (below), computers analyse the information received from the many instruments used in the air, on land, at sea and from satellites. However, computers alone cannot predict the weather – expert meteorologists also study the information in order to make good weather forecasts for several days ahead.

Air presses on us from all directions. A barometer (above) is used to measure how strong this pressure is. Damp air has less pressure than dry air, so low air pressure means there is rain about. Barometers like this have been used for hundreds of years and are still used by amateur weather forecasters today.

Balloons filled with helium gas (left) are sent over 20 km into the atmosphere, carrying instruments that measure air pressure, temperature and humidity. Information is also collected by aircraft, such as this one pictured below, which has been adapted for research. In the US, special aircraft fly into hurricanes to monitor what is happening.

The weather forecasts we see on television (left) are planned at weather centres. The forecasters try to make the information simple and clear, so that viewers can understand what is happening to the weather and prepare for it. This is especially important to people who work out of doors, such as farmers. Forecasts for the next few days are getting more and more accurate, but long-range forecasts, for months ahead, are still difficult to get right.

Two types of weather satellites orbit the Earth. Geostationary satellites always stay above the same point on the surface, photographing the changing cloud patterns below. Meteorologists work out wind speeds and directions from these photographs and can use them to track hurricanes. Polar-orbiting satellites travel from pole to pole, collecting information about temperature throughout the atmosphere and photographing the whole of the Earth's surface a section at a time.

Polar-orbiting satellite

Geostationary satellite

*Tropical cyclone
seen from space*

Glossary

Antibiotic
A medicine that kills bacteria and so cures the diseases caused by them.

Asteroid
A large rock or very small planet that orbits the sun. Asteroids sometimes get so close to Earth that they are pulled towards it by gravity and crash to the surface.

Avalanche
A mass of snow and ice tumbling rapidly down a mountain.

Bacterium
Singular of bacteria.

Black Death
Another name for the plague, a dangerous and infectious disease.

Cholera
A dangerous disease caused by bacteria found in polluted water.

Continent
A large mass of land.

Crust
The outer layer of the Earth. There are two kinds: the continental crust under the continents and the oceanic crust under the oceans.

Cyclone
Wind blowing in a circular motion. Tropical cyclones are made up of speeding winds and produce heavy rain. In the Indian Ocean area, the word cyclone refers to a tropical cyclone.

Epicentre
The point on the Earth's surface at the centre of an earthquake, directly above the focus.

Equator
The imaginary line around the middle of the Earth.

Exosphere
The outermost part of the atmosphere.

Fatal
Something which causes or results in death.

Fault
A crack in the Earth's crust.

Focus
The focus of an earthquake is the point where underground rocks start to break up and move.

Fold mountains
The type of mountains that are formed when two of the plates making up the Earth's crust push so hard against each other that they are forced upwards.

Humidity
A measure of how much moisture there is in the air. High humidity makes people feel hot and sweaty.

Lava
The name for magma when it reaches the Earth's surface.

Liquefaction
The effect an earthquake can have on soft rocks or soil – making them behave like liquid.

Magma
Molten rock from beneath the Earth's crust.

Magnetosphere
The layer of the atmosphere just below the exosphere.

Mantle
The layer of the Earth between the crust and the outer core.

Mesosphere
The layer of the atmosphere below the magnetosphere.

Meteorite
A large rock that falls from space to the Earth's surface. Meteorites often burn up on their way through the Earth's atmosphere.

Plague
A disease carried by the fleas of Black rats from Asia. The word can also be used to describe large numbers of pests.

Pressure
Continuous force against something. Air exerts pressure on the Earth and everything on it. Pressure between rocks under ground can force them to move, causing an earthquake. Pressure building up in a volcano can cause an explosion and eruption.

Stratosphere
The layer of the atmosphere above the troposphere.

Tidal wave
See tsunami.

Tornado
A whirling funnel of high-speed wind occurring on land, most often in the United States.

Troposphere
The layer of the atmosphere nearest the Earth's surface. It contains the air we breathe and it is where weather takes place.

Tsunami
A huge wave caused by an earthquake under the ocean.

Typhoon
The name for a tropical cyclone in the Western Pacific area and China.

Vaccination
A method of protecting people against a disease.

Volcano
A mountain in which material from deep below the Earth's surface escapes to the surface during an eruption.

Water vapour
Water in the form of gas. When cooled, water vapour turns back into water.